Antarctica
Land of the Penguins

Written and photographed by
Jonathan and Angela Scott

Contents

About the Authors

Jonathan and Angela Scott live in Kenya, in Africa. Their work as wildlife photographers takes them all over the world in search of rare and beautiful animals and birds. They have travelled to Antarctica many times since 1991, taking many of the pictures in this book.

What is Antarctica?

Antarctica is that magical land at the far south of the world. It's so wild and beautiful that it's hard to describe what it feels like to be there.

It is the coldest, windiest place on Earth, with temperatures as low as -89°C (-129°F). The Southern Ocean that surrounds it has larger waves and stronger winds than anywhere else on Earth.

It seems hard to believe that anything could live in such a place. However, one kind of bird survives there in large numbers – the penguin.

Antarctica is made up of the Antarctic mainland and the islands around it.

The mainland is a huge rocky land covered with snow and ice. It was the last place on Earth to be explored and no humans make it their home.

How the Arctic and the Antarctic are different

The Arctic	The Antarctic
includes the North Pole	includes the South Pole
no land, only ice floating on water	a land covered in ice
Polar bears and seals live there, but no penguins.	Penguins and seals live there, but no polar bears.

The Antarctic mainland is enormous. It is 58 times larger than the United Kingdom. In winter it doubles in size, as the sea around it freezes.

Most creatures can't survive inland during the winter. Some live on the coasts which are warmer but most move further north to escape the extreme cold. The Emperor penguin is one of the few creatures which can cope during these dark and freezing months.

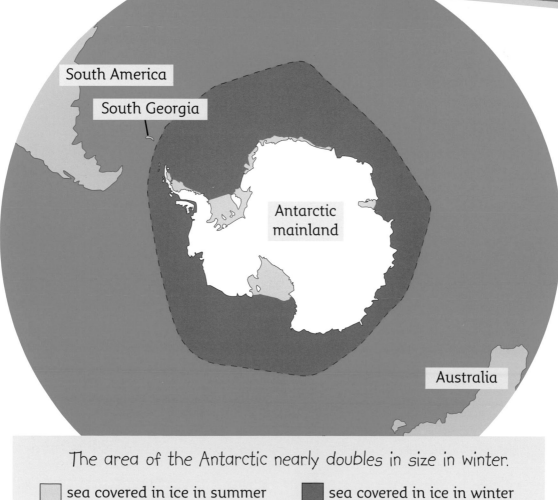

South America

South Georgia

Antarctic mainland

Australia

The area of the Antarctic nearly doubles in size in winter.

☐ sea covered in ice in summer   ◼ sea covered in ice in winter

A land of snow

If you dug down 100 metres into the snow, you would find snow that fell a thousand years ago. This snow has been pressed down and changed into ice.

Over thousands of years, the ice has built up into sheets that are over three kilometres thick. Some of this ice is half a million years old.

Buried far beneath the snow and ice, there is land.

70% of the world's **fresh water** is trapped as Antarctic ice.

In places, mountains poke through the ice.

Glaciers

Some of the ice that covers Antarctica is sliding very slowly downhill towards the sea in "rivers". These rivers of ice are called **glaciers**. Where the glaciers meet the sea they form a wall of ice.

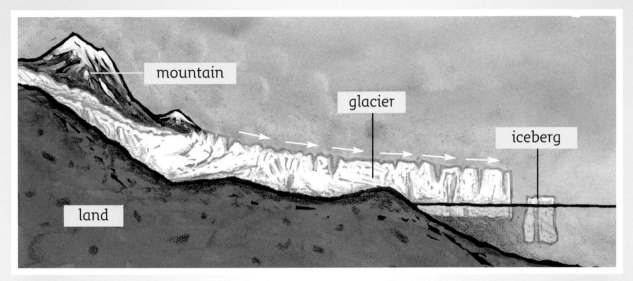

mountain

glacier

iceberg

land

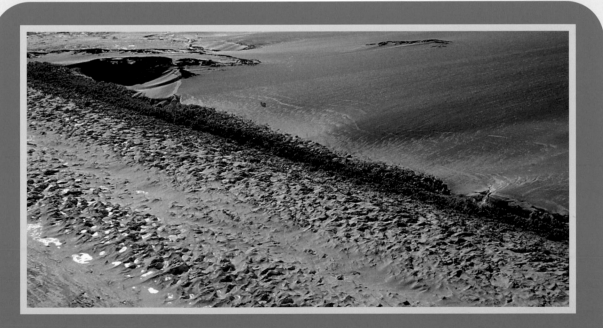

Antarctica's fastest-moving glacier is the Shirase glacier. It moves two kilometres a year. The Beardmore glacier moves just one metre a year!

Icebergs

At the coast, the peaceful stillness is sometimes **shattered** as huge chunks of ice break off from the glaciers and float out to sea. These are **icebergs**. Most of an iceberg is hidden beneath the water. Icebergs are as hard as rock and can sink a ship.

Long days and nights

The sun never rises during
the Antarctic winter and
in summer it never sets.
This is because Antarctica
is so close to the South
Pole. Exactly the same
thing happens at
the North Pole, too.

A place without trees

There are no trees in Antarctica, only **mosses**, **lichens** and
two kinds of flowering plants. These grow mostly near
the sea and on islands such as South Georgia.

These lichens on a cliff are among the few plants found in Antarctica.

Penguins

Different kinds of penguin

The best loved of all Antarctic birds are the penguins. They look like people in black suits and white shirts. They aren't afraid of visitors, and often walk right up to have a look at them.

There are many different kinds of penguin in the world. Seven of these kinds live in Antarctica.

King penguin

Gentoo penguin

Adelie penguin

Emperor penguin

Chinstrap penguin

Rockhopper penguin

Macaroni penguin

Emperor penguins are the largest kind of penguin and they weigh up to 40 kilograms. They would come up to a man's waist.

Five kinds of penguin live on the islands in the vast ocean surrounding the Antarctic mainland. South Georgia is one of these islands. The scenery is spectacular with snow-covered mountains and glaciers.

Huge colonies of King penguins live there. King penguins are almost as big as Emperor penguins but are more brightly coloured.

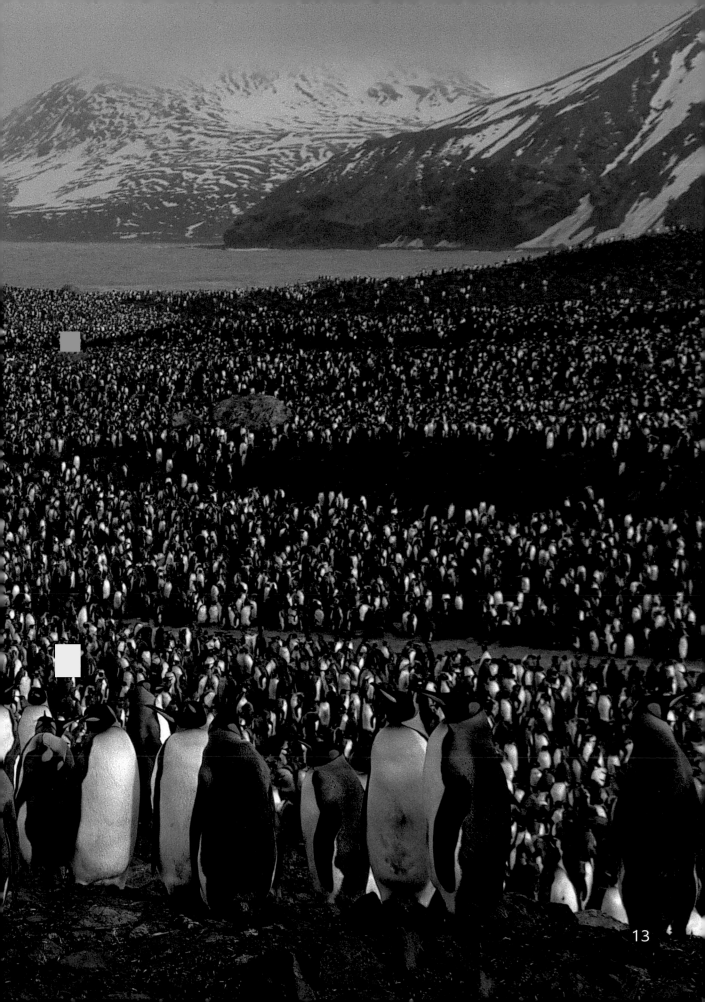

Emperor and Adelie penguins live in large colonies on the Antarctic mainland. However, only Emperor penguins can survive here in the extreme cold of winter. Adelie penguins move north onto the ice-covered sea.

an Adelie penguin colony

How penguins survive

Great swimmers

Penguins can't fly and they look clumsy and helpless on land, but in the sea it's another story. Their wings have become flippers to help them swim. In fact penguins are such good swimmers that they seem to "fly" through the water.

Penguins have to be great swimmers and divers as they get all of their food from the sea. There is nothing for them to eat on land.

King penguins can dive as deep as 240 metres in search of squid and fish.

The smaller penguins such as Adelie, Chinstrap, Macaroni and Gentoo feed mainly on krill, which are tiny creatures like shrimps.

Keeping warm

Penguins have feathers to keep them warm, just like
a duvet keeps you warm in bed. They also have a thick
layer of fat beneath their skin for the same reason.
This fat layer is called **blubber**. Whales and seals also
have blubber to keep them warm.

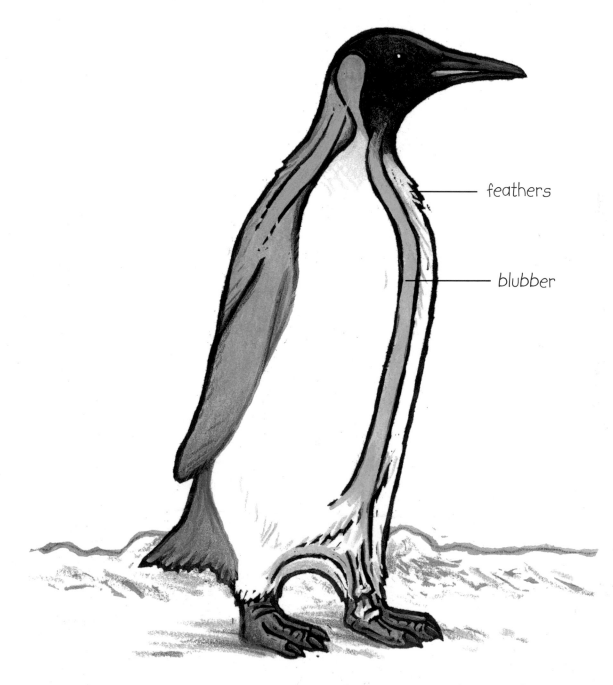

feathers

blubber

Enemies of the penguin

One reason why penguins don't need to fly is because in Antarctica there are no land animals to kill them.

That doesn't mean they don't have enemies. When penguins go into the sea they are in danger from their greatest enemy – the Leopard seal. They can also be killed and eaten by Fur seals and Killer whales (also called Orcas). Seabirds like skuas and giant petrels try to steal their eggs and kill their chicks.

A Leopard seal

King penguins chase
away a fur seal.

A skua eats a dead penguin.

In the past, explorers and hunters have also been among
the penguin's biggest enemies. They found penguins easy
to kill for food, and they also collected their eggs.

Baby penguins

Penguins lay eggs. Most penguins come back to the same nest every year. They defend their nest from other birds by pecking, kicking and hitting with their stumpy little wings.

Gentoo, Chinstrap and Adelie penguins use small stones or pebbles to make their nests, and will try to steal stones from each others' nests.

Adults feed their chicks with food they have already eaten. These Gentoo, Rockhopper and Chinstrap chicks are trying to get their parents to give them food.

Both penguin parents work together to bring up their babies. They take turns keeping their eggs warm, looking after the nest and feeding the chicks. When one of the parents comes back from a feeding trip, it greets the other noisily at the nest. Then they change places.

This is a dangerous time, as leaving the eggs or young chicks alone for a moment can let a skua nip in to steal them.

King penguins lay only one egg. They don't build a nest for it. Instead they balance it on top of their feet so that it doesn't touch the ground. A special flap of skin on the penguin's tummy, called a **brood pouch**, covers the egg and keeps the cold out.

A newborn chick huddles inside its parent's brood pouch. It takes a year for the young King penguin to grow its adult feathers. Until this happens, the chick is covered in a thick, brown coat of **downy** feathers.

Antarctic animals

There are other animals in Antarctica besides penguins.

Seals

There are six kinds of seal found in the seas around Antarctica. The most strangely named is the Crabeater seal. These don't actually eat crabs! Instead they feed mainly on krill.

They rarely come to land, spending their whole lives at sea or lying on icebergs, trying to avoid the Leopard seals and Killer whales that hunt them.

Crabeater seals are resting on the ice.

Fur seals used to be killed for their fur coats and oil. They are very fast swimmers, and at times they leap clear of the water, so they can travel even faster.

Other Antarctic seals include the huge Elephant seal, the beautiful Weddell seal and the penguin's worst enemy – the Leopard seal.

An Elephant seal roars.

A Weddell seal enjoys a rest.

Whales

Whales aren't fish; they are **mammals** like us. They give birth to live babies which feed on their mother's milk. They are the biggest mammals in the world: a Blue whale can weigh over 100 tonnes. Many whales spend the summer in Antarctica feasting on the huge swarms of krill.

Most kinds of whale do not kill seals or penguins – but Killer whales do. They are clever hunters and can even kill other whales.

A Humpback whale dives.

Killer whales hunt in groups called pods.

The white continent

Nobody owns Antarctica – it belongs to everybody, including you. One day you may be lucky enough to visit Antarctica yourself. Then you will have a chance to see the penguins, those very special birds who survive in the coldest land on Earth.

Glossary

blubber	a layer of fat under the skin, which helps to keep some animals warm
brood pouch	a flap of skin on a penguin's tummy which folds down over an egg, keeping it warm
downy	very soft and fluffy
fresh water	water that is not salty
glaciers	rivers of ice that move very slowly downhill
icebergs	big pieces of ice floating in the sea
krill	tiny sea creatures that look like shrimps
lichens	strange plants that are part plant, part fungus
mammal	an animal that gives birth to live babies and feeds its young with milk from the mother's body
mosses	small plants that grow in damp places and have no flowers
Orca	another name for a killer whale
shattered	broken into pieces

Factfile: Antarctic penguins

	Penguin	Weight
	Rockhopper	2–4 kg
	Adelie	4–5 kg
	Chinstrap	4–5 kg
	Macaroni	5–6 kg
	Gentoo	5–8 kg
	King	10–20 kg
	Emperor	20–40 kg*

* How much an Emperor penguin weighs depends on when you weigh it! It can lose up to half its body weight just by guarding an egg, because it can't hunt food for itself.

Height	Food	Where found
45–55 cm	mostly krill	Sub-Antarctic islands**
70 cm	mostly krill	Antarctic mainland and Sub-Antarctic islands**
70–75 cm	mostly krill	Antarctic mainland and Sub-Antarctic islands**
70 cm	mostly krill	Sub-Antarctic islands**
75–90 cm	fish and krill	Antarctic mainland and Sub-Antarctic islands**
90 cm	fish and squid	Sub-Antarctic islands**
120 cm	fish and squid	Antarctic mainland

** the islands surrounding the Antarctic mainland

Visit Antarctica

The magical land at the far south of the world

See:

- seven kinds of penguin, including Gentoo, Adelie, Emperor and Macaroni penguins

- an amazing variety of whales and seals

Enjoy:

- **the sun shining at midnight**

- **spectacular icebergs and glaciers, including the Shirase glacier**

How to get there:

- **Fly to Ushuaia in Argentina**

- **Catch a boat to Antarctica for the trip of a lifetime!**

Visit www.bestantarctictours.co.ant for more details.

Ideas for guided reading

Learning objectives: use contents to find way about text; read information passages and identify main points of text; make simple notes from non-fiction texts, e.g. key words and phrases, page references; write simple non-chronological reports; explain a process or present information.

Curriculum links: Geography - Where in the World Is Barnaby Bear? Passport to the World

Interest words: Antarctica, penguin, Arctic, Emperor penguin, glacier, iceberg, moss, lichens, King penguin, Gentoo penguin, Adelie penguin, Chinstrap penguin, Rockhopper penguin, Macaroni penguin, krill, blubber, brood pouch, seal, Orca, giant petrel, Crabeater seal, Leopard seal, skua, Elephant seal, Weddell seal, mammals

Word count: 1,309

Resources: globe, whiteboard

Getting started

This text can be read over two guided reading sessions.

- Show the children a globe and ask them to locate the Arctic and Antarctic. Ask what facts they already know about both places and draw a KWL grid on the whiteboard (*what they **K**now, what they **W**ant to know and what they **L**earned*).

- Show the children the book and ask them to say what it is about from the cover and blurb. Is it a fiction or non-fiction book? How can they tell?

- Ask each child to say what they want to find out from the book and add to the KWL grid. They could then look at the contents page and choose a section accordingly. Ask each child to skim-read the section they turn to, and discuss what they find there. Encourage them to point out any new and interesting words they find, for example *glacier, iceberg, blubber*. Add any new points of interest to the grid.

What I know (K)	What I want to know (W)	What I learned (L)
Antarctica and the Arctic are very cold and snowy.	Are penguins found in both places?	Penguins live in Antarctica but not the Arctic.